# Marcel Duchamp's *Fountain*
# In Context

## Readymades
## Read and Made
## Part 2

*Lyn Merrington*

ISBN: 978-0-6487276-2-0

DEDICATION

Noel

Fountain in Context

# Contents

# Fountain in Context

# Acknowledgements

I would like to thank the University of Western Australia for its support and thank the University of Lille 3 for giving me exposure to living French language from 2003 to 2009.

I'd also like to thank all my French Friends, you know who you are, including the *petites grenouilles*, who have brought the language to life, with expressions that are not in dictionaries.

I'd like to thank my family for putting up with my seemingly permanent piles of books, and with my persistently imposing my French folly on them.

Thanks again to Professor Ian McLean.

# 1

# CON-TEXT

Marcel Duchamp's *Fountain* was considered to be the most influential work of the art of the twentieth century in a 2004 survey of 500 of the most powerful art-world figures run by the Turner Prize sponsor, Gordon's Gin[1]. Leading dealers, critics, artists and curators had been asked to choose from a list of twenty nominations. Duchamp's *Fountain*, with 64 percent of the vote, was well ahead of Picasso's *Les Demoiselles*

---

[1] Denis Dutton, *The Art instinct, Beauty, Pleasure and Human Evolution*, (New York, Berlin, London: Bloomsbury Press, 2010) 193. Dutton states the survey led to some confusion with CNN claiming Fountain had been chosen as 'the best piece of art', and the BBC railed against the choice.

*D'Avignon*, then *Warhol's Marilyn Diptych*, Picasso's *Guernica and* Matisse's *the Red Studio*. These were followed by work by Beuys, Brancusi, Pollock, Judd and Moore. *Fountain* is the most cited of Duchamp's 'works' and has had an enormous influence on the art and art figures of the Twentieth Century, and even on the art of the Twenty First century. However, the background from which *Fountain* emerged is not so well known, particularly the linguistic and literary background, which was so important for Marcel's development and approach to his creative work. This study will begin to rectify some of these lacunae.

The context in which Fountain was created, or more specifically, from which it emerged, is required to fully understand Duchamp's reasoning and its impact.

In 1917 in New York the Society of Independent artists decided to hold their first exhibition with 'No Jury –No Prizes, no commercial tricks' into which all artists were invited to enter, and their work was to be exhibited as long as the $1 initiation fee and the \$5 annual dues were paid[2]. The directors included George Bellows, John Covert, Katherine Dreier, Marcel Duchamp, Rockwell Kent, John Marin, Man Ray, Morton Schamberg, and Joseph Stella.[3]

The exhibition was to run from April 11 to May 6 1917. Duchamp was the president of the hanging committee and decided on the format for the installation of the exhibition. He opted to hang the paintings in alphabetical order, a decision which was criticised as 'pictures by the mile, hung in a go-as-you-please manner, in alphabetical order, instead of the order of merit.'[4] The letter chosen to begin with (ostensibly drawn from a hat) was the letter R[5]. It's tempting to read this as another of

---

[2] Thomas Girst, *The Duchamp Dictionary*, (London: Thames and Hudson, 2014)75, cited from Steiglitz, 'Letter to the editor', *The Blindman*, 13 April, 1917, 15.
[3] Dawn Ades 'Introduction' *3 New York Dadas and the Blind Man*, (London: Atlas Press, 2013)10,11.
[4] Elena Filipovic, *The Apparently Marginal Activities of Marcel Duchamp*, (Cambridge Massachusetts, London, MIT Press) 81. Anonymous, 'The Society of Independent Artists Exhibition at Grand Central Palace', New York Times, April 11, 1917, also cited from Camfield, *Fountain*.
[5] Filipovic, 81

Duchamp's jokes, the letter R being a homophone of the French word for art, *art*. Duchamp plays with this letter and its homophones all through his oeuvre[6].

A urinal placed on its back was entered and the fee paid. It was signed, R Mutt, and dated 1917, on the left side. This 'work' was entitled *Fountain*. A meeting of the committee ensued and during the subsequent heated discussion it was decided that it the urinal was not art and would not be exhibited. Duchamp resigned from the committee in protest. Katherine Dreier, one of Duchamp's staunchest supporters, though not present at the meeting, did plead with Duchamp to accept their decision and expressed her consternation and lack of understanding, even though she suspected it may be a joke.[7]

---

[6] For more context please see Lyn Merrington, 'Marcel's Blagues: Duchamp's linguistic Jokes' *Australian and New Zealand Journal of Art*, Vol 20, 2020 Issue 2 (upcoming) https://doi.org/10.1080/14434318.2020.1837372 and Lyn Merrington, *Readymades Read and Made: Marcel Duchamp's linguistic strategies and Jokes Part 1, 1912-1916*, (Perth: Are Press, 2019)
[7] Ades, 2013, 11.

# 2

# R MUTT

A large part of the suspicion that the Fountain was a joke was linked to the signature R Mutt.

Duchamp's own description of the event makes his jokey intention clear:

"Mutt comes from Mott Works, the name of a large sanitary equipment manufacturer. But Mott was too close so I altered it to Mutt, after the daily cartoon strip 'Mutt and Jeff' which appeared at the time and with which everyone was familiar. Thus from the start there was an interplay of Mutt: a fat little funny man and Jeff: a tall thin man... I wanted any old name. And I added Richard, [French slang for moneybags] that's not a bad name for a *pissotière*. Get it? The opposite of poverty. But not even that much just R. Mutt'[8].

There is evidence Duchamp chose a cheaper urinal than that from Mott Ironworks as the holes don't align with those in the Mott catalogue range, but rather align with one from the A.Y MacDonald Company[9]. However his jokey intent required the use of the well-known Mott brand.

The cartoon *Mutt and Jeff* was at that stage still drawn by its original creator, Bud Fischer[10]. The

---

[8] Arturo Schwarz, *The Complete works of Marcel Duchamp*, (London: Thames and Hudson, 1997) 649, cited from Otto Hahn, in 'Passport no. G255300', *Art and Artists* London, vol. 1, no.4 Jul 1966, 10. Here Duchamp has confused the two characters: Mutt is in fact the tall one and Jeff the small sidekick. See Encyclopedia.com/media/encyclopedias-almanacs-transcripts-and-maps/mutt-jeff, accessed 26/08/2020.

[9] David M Lubin, 'Opening the Floodgates', Grand *Illusions, American Art and the First World War*, (Oxford: Oxford University Press, 2016), 113. Lubin n.50, cites Kirk Varnedoe and Adam Gopnik in *High and Low Modern Art, Popular Culture* (New York, Harry N Abrams and the Museum of Modern art, 1991), 274-78 who state Duchamp 'illegitimately ennobled the object with the classier brand–name association.'

[10] Later when Fischer was making a killing from the Comic he employed others to draw it for him. Al Smith drew it from the early 30s until 1980.

strip began in 1907 with simply one character and was called A Mutt. The pronunciation of the letter *A* in French closely resembles the English pronunciation of the letter R, often leading, in Anglophone environments, to sometimes hilarious misunderstandings. Duchamp, on reading the title of the early comic strips was likely, with his French heritage, to have pronounced it as R Mutt. *Mutt and Jeff* was commonly regarded as the first successful daily comic strip. It was, in 1917, about the misadventures of two mismatched men, one tall and the other short, who had less power and influence than they pretended to have.

Duchamp's early history was, as he stated, not closely aligned with Fine Art but with cartoons:

'Remember that I wasn't living among painters, but rather among cartoonists...we associated with Willette, Léandre, Abel Faivre, Georges Huard etc. This was completely different.'[11] During his time in Montmartre Marcel was living next door this

---

[11] Duchamp in Pierre Cabanne *Dialogues with Marcel Duchamp*, (New York: Da Capo Press, 1987), 22.

7

brother Jacques Villon, who had established himself as a cartoonist since 1895, and was a regular contributor to *Le Rire, Le Courrier Francais, Chat Noir, Assiette au Beurre*, and made Cabaret posters. Marcel was successful in selling some cartoons to papers in France such as *Le Rire, Laughter* and *Le Courrier Francais, The French Mail*, from 1908 to 1910. Prior to that Marcel had participated in the *Paris Salon des Artistes Humoristes*, in 1907 and 1908[12] .

Certainly given Marcel's background the content of *Mutt and Jeff* would have appealed to him. Since their pairing in 1908 the title *Mutt and Jeff* was widely used in American culture to describe a mismatched couple. During the twentieth century *Mutt and Jeff* came to be understood in Cockney Rhyming slang: as 'deaf'. Duchamp's mother had been hard of hearing leading to many absurd misunderstandings. Given Marcel's first-hand experience of deafness the strip would have tickled

---

[12] Schwarz, 4. First published drawing Nov. 1909, the last April 1910. It was 2 years before Marcel was successful in publishing one of his cartoons.

Duchamp's fancy. The French word *malentendu*, means misunderstanding, but also literally mis-hearings emphasising the importance of aural aspects of language[13]. Further characteristics of the strip appealed to Duchamp.

The timing of the exhibition from which *Fountain* was rejected is important. The Society of Independent Artists exhibition opened on 9 April 1917, three days after America's entry into the First World War. As The American Library of Congress states, 'By having his own characters serve in the French foreign legion Bud Fischer encouraged military services on the cusp of the United States entry into World War 1.'[14]

One episode of *Mutt and Jeff* released just after this, on April 23 1917, has Mutt and Jeff in uniform. Mutt begins saying 'By Golly I'd hate to be

---

[13] *Oxford Hachette, Dictionary for Windows*, Timothy Benbow Robert Scriven, Mireille Maruin, Heloise Neefs, (Oxford, Paris: Oxford Hachette, 1994-1996) entry for *entendre, j'ai mal entendu*, I didn't hear properly, entry for *malentendu*, misunderstanding
[14] loc.gov/exhibitions/comic-art/about-this-exhibition/early-years-1890s-to-1920s/mutt-and-jeff-an-unlikely-pair/

so stupid that the Army would have to detail an officer to drill, and all by myself. Now let's see if you can obey this command.' Mutt tells Jeff 'Right about face.' Jeff turns around and proceeds to write on the wall. To Mutt's consternation at Jeff 'writing that nonsense when I'm trying to drill you' Jeff replies 'Well, I wrote about your face'. These men are not only dressed in uniform but in that of the French foreign legion. The juxtaposition of two evidently silly men in the French foreign legion uniform and Duchamp's love of the absurd, particularly in relation to linguistic slippage, puns and homophones, would have been sure to make Duchamp chuckle.

Duchamp's own experience of the military had been by his own account not positive: 'I got a job in the French military mission. Not being a soldier I was simply a captain's secretary, which I assure you wasn't at all funny. It was horrible; the captain was an idiot. I worked there for six months and then, one day, I just walked out, because making thirty dollars a week wasn't worth it.'[15]

David M. Lubin has eloquently and thoroughly reframed *Fountain* as an anti-war statement. He cites Gabrielle Buffet-Picabia, the woman with whom Duchamp had been infatuated and had travelled from Munich to see, unbeknownst to any of his circle, after his break with his brothers in 1912. She says of her April 1915 arrival in New York with her husband Francis Picabia 'No sooner had we arrived than we became part of a motley international band which turned night into day, conscientious objectors of all nationalities and walks of life living in an inconceivable orgy of sexuality, jazz and alcohol... an enraged propaganda filled the air... Seen from Broadway, the massacres in France seemed like a colossal advertising stunt for the benefit of some giant

---

[15] Pierre Cabanne, *Dialogues with Duchamp with an appreciation by Jasper Johns*, reprint of 1979 Editions Belfond London Edition (New York: Da Capo Press, 1987), 52.

corporation[16].

Lubin sees the bohemian atmosphere of Duchamp's circle as a precursor for the desperate screwing of soliders before they faced the very real possibility of death. Elsewhere Buffet-Picabia describes Duchamp, who was exempted from military duty due to a heart condition during his time in New York: 'Leaving his almost monastic isolation he flung himself into orgies of drunkenness and every other excess' She continues: 'But in a life of license as of asceticism he preserved his consciousness of purpose; extravagant as his gestures sometimes seemed, they were perfectly adequate to his experimental study of a personality disengaged from the normal contingencies of human life. He later recognised ... that in this fabrication of his personality he was very much influenced by the manner of Jacques Vaché...In art he was interested only in finding new formulas with which to assault the tradition of the picture and of

---

[16] David M Lubin, "Opening the Floodgates", Grand *Illusions, American Art and the First World War*, (Oxford: Oxford University Press, 2016, 113.

painting: despite the pitiless pessimism of his mind, he was personally delightful with his gay ironies. The attitude of abdicating everything, even himself which he charmingly displayed between two drinks, his elaborate puns, his contempt for all values, even the sentimental, were not the least reason for the curiosity which he aroused, and the attraction he exerted on men and women alike. Utterly logical he soon declared his intention of renouncing all artistic production'...'When asked to participate in artistic events, he consented only for the sake of the scandal that might be provoked'[17]

Jacques Vaché was a French writer of Anglo-Irish background known for his antimilitarism, even before the declaration of war in 1914, for his idea of interior desertion and obeying only his law of

---

[17] Gabrielle Buffet-Picabia, cited from Robert Motherwell, *The Dada Poets and Painters*, (New York: George Wittenborn Inc, 1951), 259,260. Gabrielle did become Duchamp's mistress from 1920, for three months in New York and then in Paris for three years following, see Larry Witham, *Picasso and the Chess Player*, (Hanover, London; University Press of new England, 2013), 138.

*umour, humour* without an h. Incidentally the h is not pronounced in the French word *humour*, so Vaché is making an English speaker's joke about French pronunciation here.[18]

Vaché wrote to André Breton 'Art is a stupidity, almost nothing is a stupidity, art must be something funny and a bit boring, that's all. Besides art doesn't exist'[19] In 1943 Breton declared that Vaché was 'the man he loved most in the world' though Vaché had died in 1919 of an opium overdose[20]. Vaché introduced Breton to the art of Alfred Jarry, one of Duchamp's favourites and was

---

[18] www//jacquesvache.fr/en/index.html Vaché had died in 1919, with a friend from an opium overdose.

[19] Jacques Vaché, *Lettres de Guerre*, (Paris, Eric Losfield, 1970), 60, also at http:/www:patrimoine,lorinet.bzh.histoire/personnalites/v/vache-jacques/ *'L'art est une sottise, Presque rien n'est une sottise- l'art doit etre une chose drôle et un peu assommante- c'est tout [...] D'ailleurs – L'art n'existe pas, sans doute'*

[20] Vaché was found dead in 1919 with a friend after having ingested opium, due to a lack of smoking implement. He was experienced with opium, and his death at the time was treated as an accident. See www:patrimoine,lorinet.bzh.histoire/personnalites/v/vache-jacques/ However Breton later called it a suicide as Vaché had said when he died he would not die alone, and would die in his own time.

extremely influential on him.

David M Lubin's study of *Fountain* is thorough and convincing. He relates the *Fountain* to Belgium's *Manneken Pis*, a pissing boy who saved the city by pissing on a lit fuse. However Duchamp is more passive. Lubin gives the context of Duchamp's move to the United States. Duchamp said:

I came over here not because I couldn't paint at home, but because I hadn't anyone to talk with. It was frightfully lonely. I am excused from service because of my heart. So I roamed about all alone. Everywhere the talk turned upon war. Nothing but war was talked about from morning until night. In such an atmosphere, especially for one who holds war to be an abomination, it may readily be conceived existence was heavy and dull ... From a psychological standpoint I find the spectacle of war very impressive. The instinct which sends men marching out to cut down other men is an instinct worth careful scrutiny. What an absurd thing such a conception of patriotism is! ... Personally I must say I very much admire the act of facing the approaching war with folded arms.'[21]

Lubin describes *Fountain* as 'much more than an intellectual puzzle, a corrosive undermining of Western foundational values, or a spirited *blague*, though it was certainly those things too. It was the excrescence of the nihilism bred in those, such as Duchamp and his fellow refugee artists who had managed to escape the war's tentacular reach...*Fountain* was the insolent response of a resident alien to his adopted homeland's vulgar and disgusting embrace of war...'[22] or more simply 'Duchamp's urinal nonetheless howled at the flushing of millions of lives and countless dreams down the collective toilet.'[23]

Lubin sees in the name R Mutt a reference to mongrels and mutton and [You] r mutton: a

---

[21] Lubin, 112, cited from 'French Artists spur on an American Art', *New York Herald Tribune*, Oct 24 1915, section 4 2-3, reprinted in Rudolf E. Kuenzli, *New York Dada*, (New York; Willis Locker and Owens, 1986,) 133-134,

[22] Lubin, 113.

[23] Lubin, 137. Given the general vulgarity of Duchamp's oeuvre it would be extremely difficult to read *Fountain* as an objection to vulgarity.

suggestion of sheep trudging off to slaughter in the war.

Certainly Duchamp despised war and was nihilistic, however his nihilism was not only the product of the war, but belonged to a longstanding tradition of nihilism, which I will outline further in this essay.

In returning to the signature R Mutt we see there have been many interpretations of Duchamp's intent and of the linguistic possibilities:

Rosalind Krauss suggested to Duchamp himself that R Mutt was a homophonic reference to the German word *armut,* meaning poverty. *Armut* is sometimes used to describe intellectual poverty, however, when asked, he denied this[24]. As Cevizli indicates, the juxtaposition between the French nickname *Richard*, slang for moneybags, and the German

---

[24] Antonia Gatward Cevizli, 'R. Mutt's Fountain: Art Literally turned pear shaped', *Canadian National Gallery Review*, Vol 9. Issue , May 2018, 50-53 https://doi.org/10.3138/ngcr.9-004, cites Otto Hahn, 'Marcel Duchamp interviewed" In *Duchamp Passim: A Marcel Duchamp Anthology,* Ed Anthony Hill, (Basel: Gordon and Breach, 1994), 69.

*armut* for poverty, or when pronounced phonetically *Riche armut*, Rich poverty, seems too great a coincidence if he were simply searching for 'any old name' as he claimed. Once again Duchamp's understated slyness slips in paradox and lets us decipher the details. He gives us the nonsense of sense.

Antonia Gatward Cevizli suggests R Mutt references the Turkish word for Pear *armut* and in submitting it to the exhibition Duchamp 'turned the idea of art pear shaped, both literally and figuratively.'[25]

As Girst indicates elsewhere, there are several further puns implied by the name R Mutt. He gives a reversal, as in the common French slang, *verlan*, which is formed by inverting the syllables. *Verlan's* own name is a phonic reversal of *l'envers*, meaning reversal or the wrong way.'[26] R Mutt, Mutt R, pronounced in English gives mutter. As Girst is

---

[25] Gatward Cevizli, Perhaps this is so, however there is no evidence Duchamp had any knowledge of Turkish. Nevertheless he would have delighted at the use of an idiomatic expression in this way.

[26] Oxford Hachette *verlan*: French slang formed by inverting the syllables.

German he also reads here the German word for mother, *Mutter*. This is quite a plausible implication on Duchamp's part as he had spent some time in Munich immediately after his break with the Cubists in 1912. Girst also sees a similarity with the German word for checkmate, Mutt, *Matt*, implying Duchamp has checkmated the committee by indicating the deficiency of their rules with *Fountain*.

As R stands for Richard, a common French nickname for a rich person, Girst reads *Richard* in an expanded approximation or a paronymic pun in French pronunciation: *Rich art* + Mud. Girst sees in this a reflection of Duchamp's distaste for the monetisation of art[27].

All these paraphonic and homophonic resonances and spoonerisms reveal the possible permutations of a name, a signature, and show the slipperiness of language and definition, with which Duchamp so loved to play.

---

[27] Girst, 125.

# 3

# RESIGNATION AND FALLOUT

Duchamp's resignation from the committee was reported in the papers, and Duchamp noted in a letter to his sister Suzanne that it was perhaps '*un potin*', a juicy piece of gossip in New York, however its impact was not felt until much later[28].

At the request of Roché, Covert, Miss Wood, Duchamp and Co.' the urinal was taken off site, and skilfully photographed by Alfred Steiglitz in his

---

[28] Duchamp *Affect Marcel, The Selected correspondence of Marcel Duchamp*, Eds, Francis Naumann, and Hector Obalk, translated Jill Taylor, London: Thames and Hudson, 2000, 47.

gallery[29]. Beatrice Wood describes him as taking 'great pains with the lighting', such that a shadow suggested 'a veil.'[30] He positioned it against a painting by Marsden Hartley entitled *The Warriors*, as a symbolic statement against "bigotry in America."[31]

Lubin has contextualized Steiglitz's support of Hartley and the use of his work in relation to Steiglitz's German heritage and his pacifist leanings, despite his declaration that 'the War... is a most wonderful thing' that would sweep away outworn traditions. Hartley's work, created in the pre-war Berlin, glorifying German soldiers on horseback has homoerotic overtones and was not well received when it was exhibited at Steiglitz' gallery. Lubin sees in Steiglitz' photograph a fusion

---

[29] De Duve, *Kant After Duchamp*, MIT Press, 1996, citing Steiglitz's words to The Sun's critic Henry McBride in Naumann, "The Big Show", Part 1, 39, no.22

[30] De Duve, 117, citing Beatrice Wood, *I Shock Myself*, 30. Reprinted in *Three New York Dadas and the Blind Man*, Atlas Press, Introduction by Dawn Ades, (London, Atlas Press), 154-175.

[31] De Duve Cites William Camfield, in reference to an unpublished letter from Steiglitz to Georgia O'Keefe.

of New York, Berlin and Paris at a time when nationalistic sentiment was rising and neutrality was not an option.[32]

De Duve has indicated that the choice of Steglitz to photograph the *Fountain* was a strategic gesture. Duchamp could have had his friend Henri-Pierre Roché or another photographer document the *Fountain*, but Stieglitz was responsible for the magazine *Camera Work*, had launched photographers, exhibited important European artists and was 'the maker of the American Avant Garde'. He was exterior to Duchamp's circle and his role in raising the status of photography to that of art was significant.[33]

Steiglitz looked forward to a new artistic future. His letter, published in the second issue of *The Blindman*, supporting what he called the Independents' chief function: 'the desire to smash antiquated academic ideas.' He suggested that the next Independents' exhibition should 'withhold the

---

[32] Lubin, 129
[33] De Duve, 117,118

names of the makers of all works shown'..[so that] 'each bit of work would stand on its own merits'... 'dealing a blow to the academy of commercialising names. The public might gradually see for itself,'[34]

*The Blindman* was a short-lived journal edited by Beatrice Wood, Henri Pierre Roché and Duchamp. The first Edition of *The Blindman,* April 10 1917, was created to accompany the Society of independent Artist's exhibition in its first issue[35]. In the second issue, dated May 1917, an article entitled the "The Richard Mutt Case", written by Beatrice Wood and another, "the Buddha of the Bathroom" by Louise Norton, were published in support of the mysterious Mr Mutt.

Apart from the withdrawal of the entry and Duchamp's resignation, the *Fountain* was forgotten until the 1960s, when Duchamp began to be seen as the father of many art movements: the Daddy of dada the Poppa of Pop, etc. and when interest was

---

[34] Steiglitz letter addressed to 'My Dear Blindman', *The Blind Man*, Vol 2, 15, reprinted in *Three New York Dadas*, 145
[35] Girst, 28.

increasing in the *readymades* and in his oeuvre.

There has been some dispute about Duchamp's authorship as Duchamp did not lay claim to the *Fountain* until very late, and his correspondence to his sister Suzanne does not help to clarify the matter. He said:

'one of my [female] friends under a male pseudonym, Richard Mutt, sent in a urinal as a piece of sculpture'[36] This would suggest Duchamp was not the author. What reason would he have to lie to his sister Suzanne about this? She was in France and was not in contact with anyone who had any influence in the New York art scene.

---

[36] Duchamp *Affect Marcel: The Selected Correspondence of Marcel Duchamp*, Eds. Francis Naumann and Hector Obalk, translated Jill Taylor, (London: Thames and Hudson, 2000), 47. *'Une de mes amies sous un pseudonyme masculine, Richard Mutt, avait envoyé une pissotière en porcelaine comme sculpture'* The citation continues: *...aucune raison pour la refuser. Le comité a décidé de refuser d'exposer cette chose. J'ai donné ma démission et c'est un potin qui aura sa valeur dans New York.*

Louise Norton is most often named as the possible author, as her address is visible on the tag attached to the *Fountain* in Steiglitz's photo.[37] Norton's letter in support of R Mutt cites the French symbolist poet and critic Remy de Gourmont, and the philosopher Michel Montaigne, which demonstrates a profound knowledge of French culture, perhaps aided by Duchamp and Roché. Norton asks 'is he serious or is he joking, ... Perhaps he is both ... there is among us today a spirit of "blague" arising out of the artist's bitter vision of an over-institutionalized world of stagnant statistics and antique axioms.'[38]

---

[37] See Tate Museum's notes on the *Fountain* www.tate.org.uk/art/artworks/duchamp-fountain-t07573 Beatrice Wood claimed to have written the article "The Richard Mutt Case" that appeared in the *Blindman* defending the Fountain, Norton is thought to have 'sent,' as in Duchamp's letter, the Fountain, perhaps at Duchamp's behest.

[38] *The Blind Man*, vol 2, May 1917, 6, reproduced in Dawn Ades Alistair Brotchie, *Three New York Dadas and The Blind Man*, (London, Atlas Press, 2013) 136. Remy de Gourmont collaborated with one of Duchamp's other favourites, Alfred Jarry on the journal *l'Ymagier* from 1893-4. He was such a great literary critic that Eliot described him as 'the critical conscience of his generation.' One of his novels is entitled *Les Litanies de la Rose*. He was interested in sound, rhythm, Medieval

Some commentators suggest the Baroness Elsa Von Freytag Loringhoven was the author of the Fountain as she was known for her outrageous behaviour and her use of multitudinous bits and bobs, including plumbing for the creation of her artworks. The most notable of these is a work is called *God*, which was a plumbing S bend turned onto itself. This work no longer exists and is known from a print image of it.[39]

Duchamp only claimed ownership of the *Fountain* after the Baroness' death, and after the death of its photographer, Alfred Steglitz.[40] Spalding and Thompson claim this information has been in the

---

Latin literature. Michel Montaigne was a renaissance philosopher who created the essay form and favoured knowledge through experience rather than erudition, despite his erudition.

[39] Photographer Morton Livingston Schamberg, commons.wikimedia.org/wiki/file:Mortono)Schamberg_-_"God"_By Baroness_Elsa_von_Freytag-Loringhoven_and_Morton_Schamberg_-_Google_Art_Project.jpg

[40] See Glyn Thompson, Julian Spalding, "Did Marcel Duchamp Steal Elsa's Urinal" *The Art Newspaper, International Edition* issue 262, 3 Nov 2014.

public domain for years.[41] These scholars claim Duchamp was motivated by envy of his brothers, hatred of the artworld and his abandonment of chess and that he reinserted himself into the artworld this way after the death of Steiglitz, the photographer of the urinal. They note, as have others, that mutt is associated with the German word *armut* used to describe poverty and, in certain contexts, intellectual poverty.[42] They also, correctly in my opinion, state that the *readymades* are rebuses which are to be read rather than looked at, following Roussel, as Duchamp himself indicated. Their claim is that too much money has been invested in the myth of Duchamp's *Fountain* for the truth of Elsa's authorship to be revealed.

---

[41] Spalding and Thompson, say this is thanks to research by William Camfield, Hector Obalk and Kirk Varnedoe. Irene Gammel, Von Freytag-Loringhoven's biographer *Baroness Elsa: Gender Dada and everyday Modernity*, (Cambridge MA MIT press, 2002), is also credited with revealing significant details.

[42] Armut *genitive, no plural (literal, figurative)* poverty, geistige Armut Intellectual poverty; *[von Mensch]* lack of intellect, https://www.collinsdictionary.com/dictionary/german-english/armut_2 accessed 6/9/2018.

A recent article by Bradley Bailey shows Louise Norton to have been in cahoots with Marcel and supports Duchamp's authorship over that or the Baroness. Norton's address was on the ticket for the Fountain and her phone number was listed as the number for Mr R. Mutt[43]. In an unpublished part of the 1972 draft for an essay for the 1973-74 Duchamp retrospective she clearly states: 'One of Marcel's apparent jests was for him no laughing matter...to test the bona fides of the hanging committee he sent in a porcelain urinal which he titled *Fountain* by R Mutt. The committee promptly threw it out and Marcel very angry promptly resigned. In the Blind Man, A little two issue magazine sponsored and Edited by Walter Arensberg and Roché he wrote his protest. I also contributed some nonsense in the case forthwith titled Buddha of the Bathroom which at least illicited [sic] Marcel's famous chuckle.'[44]

---

[43] Bradley Bailey, Duchamp's Fountain: The Baroness theory debunked" *Burlington Magazine*, 161, October, 2019, 809, cites William Camfield exhibition Catalogue, *Fountain* Houston, Menil Collection, 1989, 30.
[44] Bailey, 810.

Beatrice Woods' claimed in her memoirs to have written "The Richard Mutt case" article.[45] Her account of the events surrounding *The Blindman* journal and the unsigned Editorial about the Fountain suggest Duchamp and Roché were behind the creation of the journal, even if they were not the authors:

I was also present at the dispute about the Urinal upside-down, between Arensberg and Bellows or it may have been Rockwell Kent. Bellows said it could not be accepted. Arensberg insisted [that] the sender had given six dollars and it had to be... I published one issue of *The Blindman* with the picture of the Urinal, because Marcel and Roché, being under the French government, felt it better for their names not to appear.[46]

---

[45] Beatrice Woods, In Ades, Ed, cited Woods memoirs *I Shock Myself*, 164.
[46] Schwarz, 649, cited from letter to author from Woods, February 1964.

Many elements surrounding the Fountain make it clear Marcel was author of this gesture, above all if we take into consideration his background.

# 4

# LA FONTAINE

The name of the Fountain, in French *La Fontaine*, references one of the most internationally famous of French authors: *Jean de La Fontaine*, 1621 – 1695. His early works *Contes*, 1665-73 were racy *Tales*, which skirted the limits of moral decency of the time, but he is most well-known and was respected internationally for his *Fables 1668-1685*. The Fables were dedicated to Louis le Grand Dauphin, the six-year-old child of Louis XIV and his queen Maria Theresa of Spain[47]. The *Fables* were moral Tales usually told with reference to animals.

---

[47] The title Dauphin comes from the county of Viennois (*Dauphiné*) which was originally given to the kings son to rule. Coincidentally it also means dolphin.

The early Tales referenced the Greek Aesop, but later Tales had wider references including the Indian sage Pilpay which were probably accessed via a French translation of 1644. [48] La Fontaine's *Fables* were a staple of French Education, often learnt by heart by primary school children.

The *Fables* were translated into English and published in several editions. One of these was published in Boston by Elizur Wright in 1841 and New York in 1859. Wright's English translation was extremely successful, six Editions being printed in 3 years. The 1843 version was produced for schools. *La Fontaine* was hence well known in the USA at the time.

The French word *fable*, means not only fable but also '*mensonge* [a lie], 'tall story'. And the idiom '*etre la fable de la ville*' means 'to be a laughing

---

[48] A Latin publication of Phaedrus' work, based on Aesop's Fables had been published in 1596 and had been very popular. In the Later Tales, La Fontaine acknowledges 'the Indian sage Pilpay'.

stock'.[49] With *La Fontaine*, the Fountain, as it is known, is Duchamp playing with us, slyly referencing an idiomatic expression which hints at his true intention? Was he intending to create a modern *fable* through his own *Fontaine*? He certainly seems to have succeeded in doing so.

Arguably Jean de La Fontaine's first 'work' happens to be the *Les Rieurs de Beau Richard*, the Laughers of Beautiful Richard. Is it just a coincidence that Richard should be the name that the author of the Fountain chose for his 'work', which questions ideas about the beautiful, *le beau* and the definitions of art?[50]

In French what in English we call the visual arts or the Fine arts are called *les Beaux arts*, literally the beautiful arts. Much of Duchamp's project consists of questioning definitions, particularly definitions of art, and often in quite contrary fashion showing them and their names to be false, misleading or

---

[49] Oxford Hachette, entry for *fable*.
[50] Beau Richard was actually a square Chateau Thierry.

simply wrong. Here in the *Fountain* Duchamp questions the definition of *Les Beaux Arts*, the beautiful arts, simply by questioning ideas of beauty.

La Fontaine's *Beau Richard* is the name of a square in Chateau Thierry where

*L'année est fertile en bon tours*,
The year is ripe with good tricks,
*'Jeunes gens, apprenez à rire'*.
Young people, learn to laugh.
*Tout devient risible ici-bas*
Everything becomes laughable here
*Ce n'est que farce et comedie*;
It's just farce and comedy
*On ne peut quasi faire un pas*,
One can almost not take a step
*Ni tourner le pied qu'on en rie*.
Or lift a foot without people laughing.[51]

---

[51] Jean de la Fontaine, "Les Rieurs du Beau Richard", https://maitrelatfontaine.fr/les-rieurs-du-beau-richard accessed 8/11/2018

*Beau Richard* is a place in which all is laughable. Furthermore, those who are the *fables de la ville*, the laughing stock, are the '*precieux*' or the affected, who '*parlent d'un certain ton*', speak in a certain tone, who '*ont un certain langage*' have a certain language, '*Dont aurait ri l'ainé Caton*, which would have made the elder Cato laugh, *lui qui passait pour un homme sage*', he who passed for a wise man.

The story of *Les Rieurs de Beau Richard* is essentially about a husband and wife who dupe a soap merchant into giving back a *cedule*, a note indicating a debt, by putting him in a difficult position where his own impropriety has led him.

La Fontaine's *Fables* are in many cases a reworking of the Greek Aesop's fables, and often centre on a moral story which was at the time a disguised criticism of the monarchy. He was well known internationally and many of his stories centre on the idea of bringing down the pretentious or revealing weaknesses and foibles.

If we look at what is rather pretentiously called the *Fountain* and describe it in plain language it is, as Duchamp referred to it, simply a *pissotière*, a urinal, or literally something that is a piss taker. As Duchamp so loved the vernacular, and idiomatic expressions it is difficult to overlook the expression as described in an American dictionary of slang 'Take the piss out of s'o- to humble someone; to make someone –usually a male,- less cocky, perhaps by violence. (Usually objectionable) you need somebody to take the piss outa you!'[52] Definitions and pretentions to deciding what was or was not art are here taken down and humbled.

Numerous expressions in French link pretentions and pissing. *'Une pisseuse'* the feminine form of the noun is 'a pretentious little twit' or a little madam'. The expression *'ne plus se sentir pisser'* –

---

[52] Richard A Spears, *McGraw's Dictionary of American Slang and colloquial expressions* (New York: 2007), 358. Although this is a contemporary dictionary the expression 'take the piss' is listed as from the twentieth century in Eric Partridge *Dictionary of Historical Slang and Unconventional English*, 8th Edition, New York: Macmillan), to pull someone's leg, 1199.

literally to no longer feel oneself pissing is used to describe someone who is, in contemporary language 'full of oneself ' or in another dictionary, 'someone who is conceited.'[53]

The verb *pisser* is also used to express value: *'ca ne pisse pas loin'* literally 'it doesn't piss far', means it has no value. Or *'pisser au cul, à la raie'*, literally piss on an arse or bumcrack, means to despise.'[54] These two expressions recall two other Duchamp works.' The first is the well known *LHOOQ*, the Q being a homophone of the word *cul*, arse or pornography, and the expression elle a chaud au cul, she has a hot arse, or is sexually aroused. The second expression *pisser à l'a raie* can be read by homophone as *pisser à l'art est..* to despise art is... This expression recalls one of Duchamp's early cartoons in which a woman is tending to her hair. The caption reads *'Que t'es long à te peigner'*, You are taking such a long time

---

[53] Oxford Hachette, entry for *pisser*, and Strutz, p. 268
[54] Mahtab Ashraf, Denis Miannay, *Dictionnaire des expressions Idiomatiques françaises*, (Paris : Usuels de Pcohe, 1995), 329

to comb your hair, to which the woman responds
*'La critique est facile mais la raie difficile'*
Criticism is easy but the parting is difficult.' This is
a pun on the expression *La critique est facile mais*
*l'art est difficile*. 'Criticism is easy but art is
difficult.

As author of the *Fountain* Duchamp is here, in
submitting an object which is clearly meant to
tests the limits of the committee's own rules for
the exhibition, reversing the roles and criticising
the critics and questioning the value of art. He is
continuing on from the lessons learned after the
1912 rejection of his *Nude Descending a Staircase*
*#2* by his peers and, most hurtfully, his own
brothers.

A urinal is usually associated with humour in both
English and French 'A pisser, urinal ...' is 'a
terribly funny joke (You laugh so hard you wet your

pants. Usually objectionable. He told a real pisser and broke up the entire class'[55]

In French similarly one says *'pisser de rire'* or *'pisser dans ses coulottes'* meaning to piss oneself laughing'[56].

Was Duchamp *'un pisse-froid'*, [a cold pisser], *un homme ... que rien ne peut emouvoir'* a man that nothing could move ?[57] He was certainly often described as such. His dry humour and love of irony were not appreciated by all.

Further expressions come to mind, certainly in relation to the *pissotière* and its reception. *'Laisser pisser les Merinos'* literally 'Let the Merinos piss', means to wait patiently.[58] Duchamp certainly had to do this as the *Fountain's* impact

---

[55] Richard A Spears, *McGraw's Dictionary of American Slang and colloquial expressions*, (New York: McGraw Hill, 2007), 268
[56] Oxford Hachette, *pisser*.
[57] Maurice Rat, *Dictionnaire des locutions françaises*, (Paris : Larousse, 1957), 311
[58] Rat, 311.

was delayed. Bernard Marcadé, Duchamp's French language biographer, has entitled a booklet thus adding the subtitle, *la paresse de Marcel Duchamp*, the laziness of Marcel Duchamp. He sees a link between the readymades *'rien faire'*, do nothing and *'laisser faire'*, let things be[59].

In returning to *Fountain*, and the author Jean de La Fontaine it is useful to indicate that many of La Fontaine's fables have entered the language in the form of idiomatic expressions which are commonly used in everyday language. They are usually tales of pretention which is revealed to be misguided.

Several of the most well-known French expressions which come from his tales are *'faire la mouche du coche'* used to describe a busybody or someone who meddles uselessly in others' affairs. This comes from the story of a fly who, in annoying the horses, and the passengers who have had to dismount from the coach believes himself to be the

---

[59] Bernard Marcade, *Laisser pisser les merinos : La Paresse de Marcel Duchamp*, (Paris: L'Echoppe) 2006.

driving force behind the coach's ascent.   The expression *'se parer des plumes du paon'*, means to dress oneself in peacocks clothing and was a warning against literary plagiarism. Another expression *'tuer la poule aux oeufs d'or*, or we would say 'to kill the golden goose', or *Lacher la proie pour l'ombre* Let go of the prey for its shadow, warn against destroying one's fortune in seeking more.[60]

La Fontaine was familiar enough with Rabelais' writings to use the name of at least one of Rabelais characters in his verse, hence the lineage from Duchamp's much-loved Rabelais is continued. [61]

---

[60] See Pierre Guiraud, *Les Locutions françaises*, (Paris, Presses Universitaires de France, 1973),34. Also Ashraf et Miannay, *Dictionnaire des expressions idiomatiques francaises*, poule 342, mouche 280, paon, 308.
[61] www.la-fontaine-ch-thierry.net/ourscomp.htm, accessed 10/11/2018, Dindenaud is a sheep merchant from Rabelais, 4th book. This name sounds suspiciously like 'didn't know' in English.

# 5

# FLAUBERT AND L'INTELLECTUEL

Many forms of the 'intellectual' have been studied in relation to Duchamp, due to his stated desire to make art an 'intellectual expression' rather than an 'animal expression', and his declaration he was tired of the expression 'stupid as a painter'.[62] However the origin of the French term *intellectuel* has not to my knowledge been sufficiently discussed. It was a key term at the turn of the century and in relation to the notorious Affaire Dreyfus, which divided France. In January 1898

---

[62] Duchamp 'The Great Trouble with Art in this Country' (1946), 117, In Gloria Moure, *Marcel Duchamp, works writings, Interviews*, (Barcelona: Ediciones Poligrafia, 2009), 115-17, also in Girst, entry for Stupid, 173

Georges Clemenceau's *'Manifeste des Intellectuels'* was the document that led to the widespread use of the term *intellectuel*. In it a group of artists and intellectuals banded together to express their consternation at the turn of events concerning Dreyfus.

Significantly, the noun *intellectuel* first appeared in a critique of the writer Gustave Flaubert, in 1882, 7 years before Duchamp's birth. Flaubert lived in the same area of Normandy as Duchamp and based his most famous novel on the town of Ry which is only several kilometres from Duchamp's home town, Blainville-Crevon. Duchamp said of his upbringing that it was 'very Flaubertian indeed' but that he didn't realise that until he read *Madame Bovary* at 16.[63]

Paul Bourget first described Flaubert as an *intellectuel* 'who plays with thought the way a child plays with poison. I think I hear in this intellectual's book, if ever there was one who has

---

[63] Duchamp in Cabanne, 19.

written the temptation, the muffled complaint, the dark sob of a victim of this cruel game of our age.'[64]

He also recognised Flaubert's nihilism, saying:

Always man arrives at a collapse of his ambition, whether it be noble or low, excessive or narrow... it s not in abstract formulae... that M Gustave Flaubert condenses this implacable nihilism. He places under our eyes concrete and living examples'[65]

---

[64] Paul Bourget originally in 'Gustave Flaubert' *La Nouvelle Revue*, 15 juin 1882, 886. Cited here from William M Johnston, 'The Origin of the Term 'Intellectuels' in French novels and Essays of the 1890s, *Journal of European Studies*, 1974, 4, 44.
 '*et il joue avec la pensée comme un enfant avec un poison. Je crois entendre dans les livres de cet intellectuel, s'il en fut qui a écrit la tentation, la sourde plainte, l'obscur sanglot d'une victime de ce jeu cruel de notre âge.*'
[65] Bourget, *toujours l'homme aboutit à un avortement de son ambition, qu'elle soit noble ou basse, démesurée ou toute étroite... ce n'est pas en formule abstraites ... que M Gustave Flaubert condense cet implacable nihilisme. Il pose sous les yeux de concrets et vivants exemples.*

Certainly in Duchamp's literary heritage the futility of pursuing beautiful dreams was a theme, and one very close to home. Perhaps it was a sentiment which resounded more strongly after Duchamp's disagreement with the cubists of 1912, and led to his abandoning groups and conventional ways of making art.

# 6

# MARCEL AND FRANÇOIS VILLON

In looking at other important figures in Duchamp's life we note François Villon, the mediaeval writer after whom his brothers Jacques Villon and then Raymond Duchamp-Villon named themselves[66].

One of François Villon's *Ballades*, known as The *Ballade du concours de Blois* begins with a line from Charles D'Orleans: *Je meurs de soif aupres de la Fontaine* , I die of thirst beside the Fountain. The *Concours de Blois* was a competition in which

---

[66] I have written in detail on the relation of Marcel Duchamp to Francois Villon and his brothers. This chapter is included in my publication *Marcel Duchamp and François Villon: Readymades Read and Made* (Perth: Are Press, 2020)

poets had to use this line as the first line of their poem. [67] Hence a tradition of paradox and contradiction was already well established, even institutionalised from the 15th century. Duchamp is firmly placed in this tradition, the lineage, tracing through his brothers who chose to name themselves after Francois Villon, to Marcel.

Villon's poem is in 3 equal verses with a refrain in the last line, following the form of Charles d'Orlean's poem. Villon's ballade, like that of D'Orléans contains a series of contradictions:

*Chault comme feu et tremble dent a dent*
I'm hot as fire, I'm shaking tooth on tooth
*En mon Païs suis en terre loingtaine*
In my own country I'm in a distant land
*Lez ung brasier frissonne tout ardent*
Beside the blaze I'm shivering in flames
*Nu comme ung ver, vestu en president*
Naked as a worm dressed like a president

---

[67] For Charles D'Orléans see
Poesie.webnet.fr/lesgrandesclassiqeus/Poemes/Charles-dorleans/je_meurs_de_soif_en_couste_la_fontaine

*Je ris en pleurs et attens sans espoir*
I laugh in tears and hope in despair
*Confort reprens en triste desespoir*
I cheer up in sad hopelessness
*Je m'esjouis et n'ay plaisir aucun*
I'm joyful and no pleasure's anywhere
*Puissant je suis sans force et sans povoir*
I'm powerful and lack all force and strength
*Bien recueully, debouté de chascun*
Warmly welcomed always turned away

*Rien ne m'est seur que la chose uncertain*
I'm sure of nothing but what is uncertain
*Obscur, fors ce qui est tout evident*
Find nothing obscure but the obvious
*Doubte ne fais fors en chose certain*
Doubt nothing but the certainties
*Science tiens a soudain accident*
Knowledge to me is a mere accident
*Je gaigne tout et demeure perdent*
I keep winning but remain the loser
*Au point du jour dis "Dieu vous doint bon soir"*
At dawn I say "I bid you good night"

*Gisant envers j'ay grant paour du cheoir*
Lying down I'm afraid of falling
*J'ay bien de quoy et si n'en ay as ung*
I'm so rich but haven't a penny
*Eschoitte attens et d'omme ne suis hoir*
I await an inheritance and am no-one's heir
*Bien recueully, debouté de chascun*
Warmly welcomed, always turned away.

*De Riens n'ay soing si mectz toute ma paine*
I never work and yet I labour
*D'acquerir biens et n'y suis pretendent*
To acquire goods I don't even want
*Qui mieulx me dit c'est cil qui plus m'attaine*
Kind words irritate me the most
*Et qui plus vray lors plus me va bourdent*
He who speaks true deceives me the most
*Mon amy est qui me fait entendent*
A friend is someone who makes me think
*D'un cigne blanc que c'est ung corbeau noir*
A white swan is a black crow
*Et qui me nuyst croy qu'il m'ayde a povoir*
The people who harm me think they help

*Bourde, verté, au jour d'uy m'est tout un*

Lies and truth today I see they're one

*Je retiens tout, rien ne sçay concepvoir*

I remember everything my mind's a blank

*Bien recueully, debouté de chascun*

Warmly welcomed, always turned away


*Prince clement, or vous plaise sçavoir*

Merciful Prince may it please you to know

*Que j'entens moult et n'ay sens ne sçavoir*

I understand much and have no wit or learning

*Parcial suis a toutes loys commun*

I am biased against all laws impartially

*Que fais je plus?Quoy? Les gaiges ravoir*

What's next to do? Redeem my pawned goods again

*Bien recueully, debouté de chascun*

Warmly welcomed, always turned away[68]


Villon's contradiction and paradox are essential to
any understanding of Duchamp's French heritage.
Many of these particular lines from François Villon

---

[68] Francois Villon, *The Poems of François Villon*, trans
Galway Kinnell, (Boston: Broughton Mifflin Company,
1977) 176-179

could have been written in reference to Marcel in his new life in the United States. Marcel was certainly aware of François Villon's work, and had internalised his spirit of contradiction and provocation.

'I die of thirst beside the Fountain'
Certainly one would die of thirst bedside Marcel's Fountain. His reorienting of the urinal by laying it on its back and renaming it ensured this.

'In my own country I'm in a distant land.'
He had adopted the United States as his own home.
'I laugh in tears and hope in despair'.
Marcel's ironic laughter was a reaction to his brothers Villon and his peers' rejection of his artwork in 1912 and the Committee of the Independents rejection in 1917, and his hope may have been in despair.

'I cheer up in sad hopelessness'.
Gabrielle Buffet Picabia's description of him reflects such an attitude 'despite the pitiless

pessimism of his mind, he was personally delightful with his gay ironies'[69]

'I'm sure of nothing but what is uncertain
Find nothing obscure but the obvious
Doubt nothing but the certainties'
Much of Duchamp's oeuvre is based on doubt, and doubt of what others considered to be certainties, such as definitions.
He said: 'Anything is dubious. It's pushing the idea of doubt of Descartes, you see, to a much further point than they ever did in the School of Cartesianism: Doubt in myself, doubt in everything. In the first place never believing in truth. In the end, you come to doubt "being".[70]

I am biased against all laws impartially.

---

[69] Gabrielle Buffet-Picabia, cited from Robert Motherwell, *The Dada Poets and Painters*, (New York: George Wittenborn Inc, 1951), 259,260.
[70] *Marcel Duchamp, Paroles D'Artistes*, (Paris, Fage Editions, 2018), 24. from Interview with William Seitz, 'What's happened to Art' originally published in *Vogue*, New York, 15 February, 1963

Gabrielle Buffet Picabia's description speaks of 'his contempt for all values, even the sentimental'[71]

The late-night chess games and partying at Arensberg's home may have led to a similar sentiment to that of Francois Villon's:
At dawn I say "I bid you good night"
'Lying down I'm afraid of falling', as one would be if drunk,
And Marcel's good fortune in finding the Arensbergs as patrons is reflected in the following line:
'I'm so rich but haven't a penny'

'I never work and yet I labour'
Duchamp didn't 'work' a regular job but laboured on his art, though not to acquire goods, as Villon had.

Certainly Duchamp would have concurred with Villon in saying
'A friend is someone who makes me think'

---

[71] Gabrielle Buffet Picabia in Motherwell, 259.

The relevance of these lines of Francois Villon's to Duchamp's life demonstrates the importance of his particular French heritage, which celebrated the vulgar, the commonplace and the larrikin, throwing doubt on institutions and parodying their forms and their thinking.

# 7

# JARRY AND RABELAIS

Despite Duchamp's avowed admiration of the demonstrably vulgar Rabelais and Jarry, the vulgar has been suppressed in reference to Duchamp studies.

Duchamp stated: 'Rabelais and Jarry were my gods evidently. They were an example to me of what could be unserious yet express things that were not completely the lowest form of wit.' [72] Clearly Duchamp loved the vulgar, and did not consider Rabelais to be the lowest form of wit, despite his

---

[72] Duchamp in Calvin Tomkins, *Marcel Duchamp: The Afternoon Interviews*, (New York: Badlands Unlimited, 2013) 86.

evident consistent vulgarity, or perhaps that statement was ironic.

Rabelais' name in the form of the Rabelaisien is used to describe language that exhibits "*exuberance, abondance, et burlesque*' or of 'earthy humour', *gai licentious, grivois, truculent*' gay, licentious, bawdy, earthy,' and is generally understood to be vulgar[73]. Rabelais was well known for his names, puns and spoonerisms which reveal a vulgar meaning. In the *1890- 1904 Dictionary of Slang and its analogues* for the word prick, meaning penis, there are more than 154 analogous French terms which are directly sourced from Rabelais[74]. This clearly identifies his love of the vernacular and his imaginative and consistent use of slang and varied language to describe the male anatomy and its functions. Inclusions in this entry

---

[73] *Le Nouveau Littré*, Editions Garnier, Paris, 2005, p.1409. and Alain Rey, *Le Robert Dictionnaire Historique de la Langue Française*, Paris, 1993, p.1697, and *Oxford Hachette Dictionary for Windows*, for translation of *grivois*. Entry for *grivois*.
[74] J.S. Farmer and W.E. Henley, *Slang and its analogues*, (New York: Arno Press, 1970 reprint of original seven volumes published between 1890 and 1904), 290-293

are 'pis (RABELAIS); pissot (RABELAIS: pissotiere+f.p.)'[75]

Alfred Jarry was an eccentric writer who was most well known for his play *Ubu Roi, King Ubu* which began with the word *Merdre*, a neologism and homophone of the word *merde*, shit, an outrageous statement for the time[76].

Duchamp's most well-known reference to Jarry is the equation he created with the homophones, *arrhes /art = merdre /merde included in his Box of 1914.* As indicated by Bert Jansen, French Dictionaries and schoolbooks regularly contained lists of homonyms. The particular *art/ arrhes* homonym is to be found in the *Grand Dictionnaire Callewaert, 1900*[77]. Here Duchamp is literally equating *arrhes*, a monetary deposit, with Jarry's

---

[75] Farmer and Henley, p.293.

[76] Alfred Jarry, *Ubu*, (Paris: Folio Classique, 1978), 31. For a comprehensive study of Jarry in relation to Duchamp see William Anastasi, "Duchamp on the Jarry Road", *Artforum*, 30, 1991, 86-90. *Art / arrhes* is note 51 in the Boite of 1914.

[77] Bert Jansen, 'More About Duchamp's wordplay', *Relief* 10, 1, 2016, 31

neologism merdre, which is a homophone of the neologism *Merde*, shit. He is equating *art* with *merde*, shit.

The common expression '*mettre quelqu'un en boite*, literally 'to put someone in a box' means to tease them or send them up, so here Duchamp is sending up his notes and himself in putting his hallowed words into a box, the originals of which he entrusted to his patron Walter Arensberg[78]. Arensberg had a fascination with deciphering hidden codes and worked 'to prove that it was Bacon who had written Shakespeare's plays.' He dedicated much time, and money to this activity, though Duchamp said of these he didn't think it had any scientific value 'I think it was the conviction of a man at play.'[79]

Five copies of the *Boite of 1914* were made. As Schwarz notes Jacques Villon's copy of the *Boite*, was inscribed *Liard*, half farthing' meaning

---

[78] *Mettre en boite*, Oxford Hachette, *boite*,
[79] Duchamp in Cabanne, *Dialogues*, 1987, 52.

worthless, and recalling the French expression '*il n'a pas un rouge liard*', the equivalent of 'he hasn't a brass farthing'. *Liard* evokes the word *l'art* perhaps implying that art is worthless[80]. Scwharz suggests the readymades were intended as a replacement for worthless art, however I tend to think Duchamp was making an ironic statement about this *Boite*, inscribing it as worthless. One's *boite* is also knows as one's office, factory or business[81]. This *Boite of 1914* was the first of Duchamp's *Boites*, in which he created replicas of his 'works.'

Duchamp's *Fountain* is a pendant to Jarry's *Ubu Roi* clearly continuing the Rabelasian lineage. Duchamp's method with the other *readymades* can be demonstrated to be systematic and consistent, using the same linguistic strategies all the way through. Some of the strategies and vulgar language he uses and his nihilism, humour and

---

[80] Schwarz, 601.
[81] Oxford Hachette, *boite*

paradox continue on from the historical literary precursors I have discussed above.

# 8

# CONCLUSION

Just as *Fountain* spouts meaninglessness and meaning, we may never know the truth. Perhaps this is the most important thing we can take from Duchamp. Definitions and rules are made to be broken. Duchamp demonstrates time and again that language is fluid, and above all ambiguous. He shows us that his 'art' does not conform to the standard art rules.

He said:
the word "art" interests me very much. If it comes from Sanscrit, as I've heard, it signifies "making." Now everyone makes something, and those who make things on a canvas, with a frame, they're

called artists. Formerly they were called craftsmen, a term which I prefer. We're all craftsmen ... The word "artist" was invented when the painter became an individual[82].

The *Readymades* demonstrate the contradictory nature of language and definition. They are evidently not 'made' by the artist. As declared in the Blindman Journal 'whether Mr Mutt with his own hands made the fountain has no importance. He CHOSE it. He took and ordinary article of life, placed it so that its useful significance disappeared under the new title and point of view - created a new thought for that object.'[83]

Duchamp used his particular French heritage to advantage, creating mystique in an anglophone environment. The fluid nature of language was reinforced every day as he learned English in an anglophone environment and taught French. Continually searching for terms in dictionaries as

---

[82] Cabanne, 16.

[83] Beatrice Wood, 'The Richard Mutt Case,' The Blindman, (New York) no.2, 5. Reproduced in Ades, 139.

his vocabulary grew highlighted the slippery contradictory, and ever-changing nature of language. But Duchamp remained very much a Frenchman. His linguistic heritage is key.

If Duchamp's art allies itself to any form it is the forms of *'umour'* and *fable*. It celebrates the vulgar, is contradictory or paradoxical, and should not be taken seriously.

Duchamp's world was one in which war loomed large, but which he managed to escape, due to his heart condition. It is not surprising that he chose *'umour'* as an escape route from the insurmountable horrors that unfolded around him.

# 9

# SELECTED BIBLIOGRAPHY

Ashraf, Mahtab, Miannay, Denis, *Dictionnaire des expressions Idiomatiques françaises*, (Paris : Usuels de Poche, 1995)

Ades, Dawn, Brotchie, Alistair, Eds., *Three New York Dadas and the Blind Man*, (London: Atlas Press, 2013)

Anastasi, William, "Duchamp on the Jarry Road", *Artforum*, 30, 1991.

Bailey, Bradley, Duchamp's Fountain: The Baroness theory debunked" *Burlington Magazine*, 161, October, 2019

Cabanne, Pierre, *Dialogues with Marcel Duchamp*, (New York: Da Capo Press, 1987)

Collins dictionary, https://www.collinsdictionary.com/dictionary/german-english/armut_2 accessed 6/9/2018.

De Duve, Thierry, *Kant After Duchamp*, MIT Press, 1996.

Duchamp, Marcel, *Marcel Duchamp, Paroles D'Artistes*, (Paris, Fage Editions, 2018)
*Duchamp du Signe*, (Paris: Champs Flammarion, 1994)
*Notes*, (Paris: Champs Flammarion, 1999)

Dutton, Dennis, *The Art Instinct, Beauty, Pleasure and Human Evolution*, (New York, Berlin, London: Bloomsbury Press, 2010)

Farmer J.S., Henley, W.E., *Slang and its analogues*, (New York: Arno Press, 1970 reprint of original seven volumes published between 1890 and 1904)

Filipovic, Elena, *The Apparently Marginal Activities of Marcel Duchamp*, (Cambridge Massachusetts, London, MIT Press)

Gatward Cevizli, 'Antonia R. Mutt's Fountain: Art Literally turned pear shaped', *Canadian National Gallery Review*, Vol 9. Issue, May 2018, 50-53

Girst, Thomas, *The Duchamp Dictionary*, (London: Thames and Hudson, 2014)

Guiraud, Pierre, *Les Locutions françaises*, (Paris, Presses Universitaires de France, 1973

Fontaine, Jean de la, "Les Rieurs du Beau Richard", https://maitrelatfontaine.fr/les-rieurs-du-beau-richard accessed 8/11/2018 www.la-fontaine-ch-thierry.net/ourscomp.htm, accessed 10/11/2018

Jansen, Bert, 'More About Duchamp's wordplay', *Relief* 10, 1, 2016, 30-69.

Jarry, Alfred, *Ubu*, (Paris: Folio Classique, 1978)

Jeff and Mutt
Encyclopedia.com/media/encyclopedias-almanacs-transcripts-and-maps/mutt-jeff, accessed 26/08/2020.
loc.gov/exhibitions/comic-art/about-this-exhibition/early-years-1890s-to-1920s/mutt-and-jeff-an-unlikely-pair/

Johnston, William M, 'The Origin of the Term 'Intellectuels' in French novels and Essays of the 1890s', *Journal of European Studies*, 1974, 4, 44.

*Le Nouveau Littré*, Editions Garnier, Paris, 2005

Livingston Schamberg, Morton,
commons.wikimedia.org/wiki/file:Mortono)Schamberg_-_"God"_By Baroness_Elsa_von_Freytag-Loringhoven_and_Morton_Schamberg_-_Google_Art_Project.jpg

Lubin, David M, 'Opening the Floodgates', Grand *Illusions, American Art and the First World War*, (Oxford: Oxford University Press, 2016) 109-139

Marcade, Bernard, *Laisser pisser les merinos : La Paresse de Marcel Duchamp*, (Paris: L'Echoppe) 2006.

Merrington, Lyn, 'Marcel's Blagues: Duchamp's linguistic Jokes' *Australian and New Zealand Journal of Art*, Vol 20, Issue 2, 2020
https://doi.org/10.1080/14434318.2020.1837372
Merrington, Lyn. *Readymades Read and Made: Marcel Duchamp's Linguistic Strategies and Jokes Part 1, 1912-1916*, (Perth: Are Press, 2019)
*François Villon and Marcel Duchamp: Readymades Read and Made Part 3*, (Perth: Are Press, 2020)

Motherwell, Robert, *The Dada Poets and Painters*, (New York: George Wittenborn Inc, 1951)

Moure Gloria, Marcel *Duchamp: Works, Writings, Interviews*, (Barcelona: Ediciones Poligrafia, 2009)

Naumann, Francis, Obalk, Hector, Eds., *Affect Marcel, The Selected correspondence of Marcel Duchamp*, translated Jill Taylor, (London: Thames and Hudson, 2000)

D'Orléans, Charles, Poesie.webnet.fr/lesgrandesclassiqeus/Poemes/Charlesdorleans/je_meurs_de_soif_en_couste_la_-fontaine

Partridge, Eric, *Dictionary of Historical Slang and Unconventional English*, 8th Edition, New York: Macmillan, 1984)

Rat, Maurice, *Dictionnaire des Locutions Françaises*, (Paris: Larousse, 1957)

Rey, Alain, *Le Robert Dictionnaire Historique de la Langue Française*, (Paris : Robert, 1993)

Schwarz, Arturo, *The Complete works of Marcel Duchamp*, (London: Thames and Hudson, 1997)

Spears, Richard A., *McGraw's Dictionary of American Slang and colloquial expressions* (New York: 2007)

Tate Museum; notes on the *Fountain* www.tate.org.uk/art/artworks/duchamp-fountain-t07573

Thompson, Glyn, Spalding, Julian, "Did Marcel Duchamp Steal Elsa's Urinal" *The Art Newspaper, International Edition* issue 262, 3 Nov 2014.

Tomkins, Calvin, *Marcel Duchamp: The Afternoon Interviews*, (New York: Badlands Unlimited, 2013)

Vaché, Jacques, www//jacquesvache.fr/en/index.html http:/www:patrimoine,lorinet.bzh.histoire/personalites/v/vache-jacques/

Jacques Vaché, *Lettres de guerre, Précédés de 4 essais de André Breton*, (Paris: Eric Losfield, 1970) *Les Solennels*, (Paris, Editions Dilecta, 2007)

Villon, Francois, *The Poems of François Villon*, trans Galway Kinnell, (Boston: Broughton Mifflin Company, 1977)

Witham, Larry, *Picasso and the Chess Player*, (Hanover, London; University Press of new England, 2013), 138.

# Fountain in Context

# Fountain in Context

# ABOUT THE AUTHOR

Lyn Merrington is an Australian Artist and Art
Historian. She is intrigued by ambiguity, and
French language and culture. Historical research is
a mainstay of her method. As is humour.